A Fruitful Faith

A 40 Day Devotional on the Fruit of the Spirit

A Fruitful Faith

A 40-Day Devotional on the
Fruit of the Spirit

Tommy McGregor

For Wolf

TABLE OF CONTENTS

Start Here

This is a 40 day devotional. That means you need to commit to spending 40 days reading it. This also means that you should not quit if you miss a day, but instead, just pick it up where you left off. The important thing is that you read every page.

Here is what you need to do. First, plan to give yourself 20 minutes a day to work through the devotional for that day. It might not take that long every time, but you need to make sure you are not rushing through it. Secondly, you will need a pen and a Bible for every daily entry. You will be asked to look up a verse and write it in the book. You will also be asked to write your answer to one question and take a challenge. This is why you need to give yourself 20 minutes a day.

The fruit of the Spirit are characteristics of those who have committed to follow Jesus and have the Spirit of God living in them. If you have not made a decision to be a Christian, then you will need to talk to a parent or pastor before you start this book.

I hope this book will challenge you to be more like Jesus. At your age, you have so much time to grow and mature. The sooner you start, the better it will be for you when you are older. God bless you!

Day 1

A Fruity Tree

Have you ever heard of the fruit of the Spirit? Maybe you have sung a catchy song about it. The fruit of the Spirit are nine character traits of someone who is a Christian. The nine fruit of the Spirit are love, joy, peace, patience, kindness, goodness, gentleness, faithfulness, and self-control.

Think about it this way. What kinds of fruits grow on trees? You might know that apples, oranges, and mangos grow on trees but not the same tree. Apples grow on apple trees, and oranges and mangos grow on orange and mango trees, respectively. One fruit for one kind of tree. But we are different, if we are in Christ. When we begin to follow Jesus, the Holy Spirit comes into our lives to live in us. When this happens, it is like a seed is planted in us that can produce nine fruitful behaviors. Then it is up to us to help these behaviors grow and develop to be healthy in our lives. For the next 40 days, you will be learning about these nine fruits of the Spirit. I hope that at the end of this book, you will know how to live out a fruitful faith in Jesus' name.

Look up Galatians 5:22-23 and write it here:

Answer the questions below:
Why do you think God gave us these nine fruits in our lives?

Daily Challenge:
Look up these two verses about the Holy Spirit, and describe what they mean to you: John 14: 26 & 1 Corinthians 3:16.
Now, spend some time in prayer asking God to help you take this study seriously and work on developing all of the Spirit fruits in your life.

Day 2

I Love Ice Cream

What do you love? You probably love many things like your family, your friends, and some of the games you like to play. You may also even love ice cream. I love ice cream, especially strawberry ice cream. So, with such a wide range of things to love, how are we supposed to know what love really is? What is the difference in the things we like and the things we love?

In Galatians 5:22, we see that the first fruit of the Spirit is love. This probably doesn't have anything to do with ice cream. To truly learn what the real definition of love is, we need to go to the Bible. In 1 John 3:16 we find out what love is. The verse says: "This is how we know what love is: Jesus Christ laid down his life for us. And we ought to lay down our lives for our brothers and sisters." Jesus modeled the definition of love by dying on the cross. This does not mean we have to die to show love, but it does mean that love is putting others before yourself. It sometimes means giving up things that are important to you for other people. To do that, it will take the Spirit within you to motivate you to want to meet others' needs more than your own. That is love.

Look up 1 John 4:8 and write it here:

How does it make you feel to know that you are loved by
God and others in your life?

Daily Challenge:
Look up 1 Corinthians 13:4-8, and list all of the
definitions of love from this verse. Spend some time in
prayer right now as you read through this list. Pray that
God will give you each of these attributes of love in your
life.

Day 3

The Author of Love

There are many voices in the world trying to define love. Some say that love is a feeling. Some say that love is a choice. Others say that loving someone means celebrating that person as an individual. So, how are we going to know who to believe? Think about it this way. How do you know what the speed limit is on a road? Do you go by the average speed everyone is driving, or maybe the speed that you think it should be? No, we know the speed limit by what is posted on the speed limit sign. Regardless of what you think it should be, the speed limit is the number stated on the speed limit sign. The same can be true about understanding love. The Bible is like a speed limit sign because of 1 John 4:8. This verse tells us that the author of the Bible (God) is the same as love. I want you to look it up and write it down in the space below. This verse also says that we can not understand love if we do not know God. That is why love comes from the Spirit. We can not understand love without the fruit of the Spirit.

Look up 1 John 4:8 and write it here:

Other than love, what other characteristics would you use to describe God?

Daily Challenge:
First, pray about how you will love others. Then pick one person that you are close to and complete this sentence:

Because God is love and because I love _____, I

will _____.

Day 4

Unconditional Love

Do you know what unconditional love is? It is loving without conditions. When something is conditional, there is a requirement that must be met first. Making good grades in school is conditional on you doing well on the tests, homework, etc. For love to be unconditional means that you do not have to do anything to have it. Most people do not think of love as unconditional. Instead, people think that they will love someone if that person will love them back, or give them something in return for their love. God's love for you is always unconditional. He loves you regardless of how you treat Him in return. Romans 5:8 proves this best by saying that God loves us even though we are still sinners. God's unconditional love should serve as our example for how we should love other people. If we truly want to love someone in the way that we would want to be loved, then we need to develop a heart that loves unconditionally. Unconditional love will produce joy, peace, patience, and all of the other fruits of the Spirit. It all starts with unconditional love.

Look up Romans 5:8 and write it here:

Think of a time that someone loved you without conditions. Maybe you were unfair to them, and they showed fairness to you anyway. How did that make you feel? What can you learn from it?

Daily Challenge:
Think of someone in your life who is hard to love. Now, write out 3-5 examples of how you can specifically go and show this person love without conditions. Don't forget to pray first about this challenge and allow God to lead you in it.

Day 5

Loving Friends & Enemies

The Bible talks a lot about love. We are commanded to love God and love others, which pretty much includes everyone. But, just to be clear, the Bible gives us specific instructions to love those we are close to and those we do not like to be around. In Matthew 5:43-44, Jesus says this: "You have heard that it was said, 'Love your neighbor and hate your enemy.' But I tell you, love your enemies and pray for those who persecute you." In Luke 6:27, Jesus even says to do good things to those who are mean to you. So, why would Jesus tell us to love those who hate and hurt us? The reason is that in order to have a loving heart, we must love everyone regardless of how they treat us. If you only love those who are easy to love, your ability to love will not be strong enough to get you through the hardest moments of your life. Loving your friends is important to learn how to love, but loving your enemies will help you truly develop this first fruit of the Spirit.

Look up Luke 6:27-31 and write it here:

Think of a close friend who is easy to love and someone you know who might be considered an enemy. What is it about each of those two individuals that make them that way to you?

Daily Challenge:
The challenge, for the rest of your life, is to love. Make a commitment to yourself that you will do these three things every day: 1. Look at people though the loving eyes of Jesus. This means you don't judge them, but you see them for who they can be, instead of who they might be now. 2. Commit to controlling your anger towards people so that they have a hard time hating you. 3. Show kindness to everyone, no matter how they respond in return. Spend some time praying about this.

Day 6

I've Got the Joy...Where?

Did you ever sing the song: "I've got the joy, joy, joy, joy, down in my heart"? The best part of that song was yelling out "where?" after the last "joy" and before the answer: "down in my heart." That was a fun song when I was a kid, and yet it is still a good reminder of where we find joy. According to Galatians 5:22-23, the second fruit of the Spirit is joy. In the book of Psalms, David writes a lot about making a joyful noise. In Psalm 95:1 he writes, "Oh come, let us sing to the Lord; let us make a joyful noise to the rock of our salvation!" This is a call to worship, and worship should always come straight from your heart to God. One of the most famous chapters in the Bible is Psalm 100, and it is filled with joyful descriptions of worship. Many times when we express joy, we sing, dance around, and thank God for the life He gave us. The song is right: joy does come from the heart. It comes from a heart that is in sync with God in worship.

Look up Psalm 100:1 and write it here:

Think back to the last time you felt joy in your heart.
Where were you, and what were you doing? How did you
express your joy?

Daily Challenge:
The challenge today is to worship God with your joy.
Find ways to "shout for joy", not literally but in your
heart and life. Have a joyful day today. Spend a few
minutes praying for joy in your life.

Day 7

Joyfulness Doesn't Rot

What other word do you think of when you think of joy? Is it happiness? Do you think that joy and happiness are the same? Well, they are not. Both are an emotion, but one comes from your mind and the other from your heart. When you go on vacation or wake up on Christmas morning, the emotion you feel is happiness. You are excited and energized to start the activities of the day. Happiness is always fueled by something good that is happening around you. Most people are not happy when they are having a bad day. But joy is different. Joy is not based on what you are doing but on your relationship with Jesus. Joy is a fruit of the Spirit because it comes from the Spirit that lives in you when you are in relationship with God. You can have a bad day and still have joy because God is with you on those bad days. In James 1:2-3 we learn that we should have joy when we face hard times because those trials will make our faith stronger and develop perseverance. Perseverance is the will to continue on with something, and when we have joy, we have hope to keep going even when times are hard.

Look up James 1:2-3 and write it here:

Why do you think James said to have joy when facing difficult times in life?

Daily Challenge:
The challenge today is to pursue joy when things get hard. After you face a trial today, sit back and smile, and think of how this moment will help you grow. Now spend some time praying about this.

Day 8

My Name Is Joy

Do you know someone named Joy? I grew up with a friend named Joy, and she was always sad. It was kind of ironic that one of the saddest people I knew was named Joy. In Proverbs 10:28 we read this: "The hope of the righteous brings joy, but the expectation of the wicked will perish." This verse tells us that joy comes from a positive perspective of hope in life. In Christ, we have hope, and this hope is based on the truth that we know God is always with us and will never leave us. In Jeremiah 29:11, we learn that God has a plan for our life, and this plan is one of hope. When we do not seek hope, we will not find hope. As the Proverb explains, those without hope expect not to see it. Your given name may not be Joy, but when you have joy in your life, other people can not help but see that joy in you. They will begin to relate this fruit with your life, and you will be known as Joy.

Look up Jeremiah 29:11 and write it here:

Think of someone who has joy in his or her life. Describe that person. How does that joy spread to other people around them?

Daily Challenge:
Today we learned that joy comes from a hope in Christ. Think about all the things that give you hope in your relationship in Jesus. Feel free to write that list on this page of the book. Now, think about how that hope brings joy to your life. Pray that you will be someone that takes hope and turns it into joy for others to share.

Day 9

Complete Joy

In order to live a life of joy, you must understand the source of your joy. Even though we may try to have joy on our own, joy can only become complete in our relationship with Jesus. Think of it like a battery of an electronic device. The battery might last a few hours on its own, but eventually it will die. The only way to keep it charged is to plug it into the power source. When it is plugged in, the charge is complete. The same is true with joy. In 1 John 1:1-4, John the disciple reminds us of what Jesus did for us. He instructs us that we will find life in Jesus and that we need to have fellowship with God, through Christ. Then, he says, our joy will be complete. In other words, we will be fully charged with joy and will be able to go out and live in that joy. So, make your joy complete by plugging into Jesus and allowing Him to live in you.

Look up 1 John 1:3-4 and write it here:

What does it take to stay "plugged in" in fellowship with Jesus?

Daily Challenge:
Look at the things you wrote in the question above. You probably said things like reading your Bible, praying, and living as a witness for Jesus. Write down a plan for how to do those things today and everyday. After that, spend a few minutes praying for God's help in doing those things.

Day 10

Peace Power

If you could have a super power, what would it be? Some might say that they would want to fly or to have lightening speed, but I would wish for peace. Peace is a super power because it comes from God. Think about it, a super power is great because it is rare. If everyone had Superman's powers, then he wouldn't be a super man. Just like love and joy, peace does not come from our circumstances. It is not created by big smiles and hand shakes. Real peace can only be found through the Spirit living in us. In Psalm 29:11 we learn that peace comes as a blessing through the strength of God. This power gives us the ability to live in peace in this world and be at peace in this world. Here is what I mean. When we live in peace, we try to bring peace to everyone we meet. When we live at peace, we know that God is in our life and nothing can take that away from us. Outside of a relationship with Jesus, no one will ever find true peace in their life.

Look up Psalm 29:11 and write it here:

Describe what happens when you live in peace with someone else.

Daily Challenge:
Think of someone close to you, like someone in your family or a close friend. Make every effort to live peacefully with them and notice how they respond to it.

Day 11

Peace Treaty

A peace treaty is an agreement between two sides that are fighting. Once each opponent agrees that the feud needs to end, a treaty is formed to create peace. This requires both parties to make a commitment to get along. You probably have friends, or brothers and sisters, where a peace treat needs to be made. Hebrews 12:14 says that we should do everything possible to live in peace with other people. As a Christian, you have the fruit of peace growing inside of you. You are called to be holy and set apart which means you are to be different than those who do not live in Christ. Peace needs to be so important in your life that you use every opportunity to create a treaty of peace with those people in your life.

Look up Hebrews 12:14 and write it here:

Why is it so hard to live in peace with people we love and are close to (family and close friends)?

Daily Challenge:
The challenge today is to create a peace treaty with someone. Think of the first person that came to mind as you read about peace today, and think about how you will live in peace with them. Spend some time praying about it, and work through the steps you might have to take.

Day 12

Peace Maker

The fruit of peace does not only give you the ability to have peace, it allows you to be a maker of peace. In James 3:18 we learn that those who make peace will receive peace. This verse uses some farming words such as "sow" and "harvest". To sow means to plant. If you have a garden, then you will sow a seed in hopes that it will grow into something good. When the crop is ready to be picked, you harvest the things you have planted. In between the time of sowing and harvesting, you usually spend some time watering the plants and picking any weeds that might grow up around it. This verse says that we need to sow peace in our relationships so that our harvest will be peaceful. That means we need to spend time working on our relationships and do our best to model peace to others. If we do this, we will find peace in our walk with Christ and, hopefully, in our relationships as well.

Look up James 3:18 and write it here:

Why is it important to have peace in your close relationships?

Daily Challenge:
The challenge for today is to make a plan for harvesting peace. If you were planting a crop, you would need to plan your steps like putting down good soil, planting the seeds, and watering the seeds every day. Think of a few close relationships, and make a list of how you will create a peaceful harvest.

Day 13

Peace of Christ

Have you ever stood on the top of a mountain and looked down? It is an amazing view because you can see so many things that you never could see from the ground. This is how God sees the world. His view is bigger than we can understand. In Philippians 4:6-7, we are told not to worry about things, but instead, we need to pray to God and let His peace cover us. Then the verse says something awesome. It says that God's peace is greater than anything we can imagine and that His peace will protect us by guarding our hearts. God is saying to you that He is watching over you from a very high mountaintop. He says that you can trust Him to protect and take care of you. He asks that you tell Him when you are afraid and allow Him to give you peace. The peace of Christ is the only peace that will never fail you.

Look up Philippians 4:6-7 and write it here:

When have you felt the peace of Christ in your life, and how did it make you feel?

Daily Challenge:
Spend some time in prayer and ask God to cover you with His peace. Present your needs to God, and allow Him to cover you and protect you. Remember how it feels when He fills you with peace. It will not happen magically after you say "amen", but it will happen when you need it most.

Day 14

Peace Out

Over the past few days, we have been looking at peace. You can hear the word "peace" used to represent many things from ending a war to a saying for goodbye. The world tries to find a meaning for the word "peace", but it never really understands how to define it. Before Jesus died on the cross, He told His friends that He will leave them peace. In John 14:27, He reminds them that His peace is not like what the world calls peace. Then He tells them that the peace He gives will keep them from being afraid. That is the peace that you have in your heart from the Spirit. The same peace that Jesus gave the disciples, He gives to you and me. This peace is not like the peace of the world because it will always comfort and protect you. Do not ever forget that you have the fruit of peace in you and that it is the peace of Jesus. He left it for us when He left this world with a great "Peace Out!"

Look up John 14:27 and write it here:

Why do you think Jesus told the disciples just before He died to not let their hearts become troubled?

Daily Challenge:
Make a list of the differences in the world's peace and the peace of Jesus. Get someone to help you with ideas if you can not think of enough examples.

Day 15

Wait For It

How hard is it for you to be patient? Patience is something that most people struggle with. One of the reasons for this is because so many things in our lives today are instant. We can look up an answer online immediately. We can microwave something to eat in seconds that would have taken previous generations hours to make. Our culture has made waiting patiently almost unnecessary. But God still thinks that waiting is important. When we wait for something, we have hope that it will come. When we wait on God, we are putting our trust in His timing and not our own.

The Bible has a lot to say about waiting on the Lord. In Lamentations 3:25-27 we read, "The Lord is good to everyone who trusts in him, so it is best for us to wait in patience—to wait for him to save us—And it is best to learn this patience in our youth." The reason it says that you should learn patience in your youth is because the older you get, the more you will need this fruit of the Spirit to help you wait on the Lord.

Look up Psalm 40:1 and write it here:

Why do you think God would ask you to wait patiently for Him and His timing?

Daily Challenge:
The challenge for today is to wait on the Lord and His timing. Make something to remind you to wait on God. It can be a string around your wrist or maybe the word "wait" or the number 40 (for Ps 40:1) written on your hand. Create a visible reminder to be patient on God, and then act on it when you are reminded to.

Day 16

The Wise Have Patience

Do you know what it means to be wise? The Bible talks a lot about wisdom. Wisdom is learning to see things through God's eyes. This happens by reading the Bible and understanding what God's Word means. Proverbs 14:29 tells us that wisdom and patience are connected because it takes patience to gain wisdom. Think about it this way. If you have a book report and you skip through the book without reading it, you will not know it well enough to write a good report on it. That is an unwise thing to do. But if you have enough patience to read the book, then you will learn it and have the understanding to write a good report. The same is true with learning from God. God does not move on your schedule. He does not give you what you ask for exactly when you want it. He knows better and gives when the time is right. It takes wisdom to understand that and patience to wait for it. This is why patience is a fruit of the Spirit. You can not follow Jesus closely without it.

Look up Proverbs 14:29 and write it here:

Why is it so hard to be patient when waiting on God to answer a prayer?

Daily Challenge:
Think of three things you need to pray for. They can be for yourself or for others. Commit to praying every day for them, and tell God you will be patient in waiting. Write down today's date next to the request. When you feel that your request has been answered (even if God did not respond like you thought He would), write down the date of when your request was answered to see how long you waited for the Lord.

Day 17

Fight Back With Patience

When we looked at peace, we learned that the Bible calls us to be peacemakers. Now, as we talk about having patience, we need to understand that the best way to make peace is to also have patience. Let's say someone at school is being mean to you. Your first response might be to be mean back, but you know that is not what a peacemaker does. So, instead you develop patience, and you wait for that person to move on from the conflict. Then, you may be able to make up with the person or, at least, avoid more problems. Proverbs 15:18 tells us that an impatient person makes things worse, but someone with patience will calm things down. This situation makes sense because we have all seen people react to a problem and make it worse than it was before. The wise, patient person will actually calm the situation down through patience and self control. We need to fight back with patience.

Look up Proverbs 15:18 and write it here:

Think back to an augment or fight you had recently. How would patience have helped the situation from getting worse?

Daily Challenge:
Write out a plan of "attack" for how you will be patient the next time you have a conflict with someone. What will you do and what will you say? How is that different from the typical way you would handle the situation?

Day 18

Loving Patience

As you already know, the first fruit of the Spirit is love. The Bible talks a lot about love and defines it in a few different verses. One of the most famous Biblical definitions of love is in 1 Corinthians 13. In verse 4, it starts: "Love is...", which is always a good way to begin a definition. After the first two words of this passage, it then lists 16 things that love is, does, and doesn't do. The first defining trait of love in 1 Corinthians 13 is that love is patient. Patience is a very important part of loving other people because when we respect someone enough to be patient with them, we are showing them love. In Ephesians 4:2, Paul tells us to be humble and gentle as we are being lovingly patient with other people. The truth is, it is easy to be impatient with people. Without much effort, and because of our sin, we can become selfish, proud, impatient, and unloving. So, when we show patience, we are trying to overcome our sin nature and demonstrate our love for that person by being kind, humble, and patient.

Look up Ephesians 4:2 and write it here:

What are some of the things that cause you to be impatient with those you are closest to? How can you try to overcome that temptation?

Daily Challenge:
On a scale of 1-10 (10= great & 1= terrible), how would you rate your ability to be patient with others? How could you make your patience score even higher?

Day 19

Grace in Kindness

Do you know what grace is? Grace is not a fruit of the Spirit, but it is at the top of the list of Godly characteristics. Grace is the act of undeserved kindness. In other words, grace is treating someone better than they deserve to be treated. If someone is mean to you and you show them kindness in return, your kindness is shown through grace. If you have a project due at school and you miss the deadline to turn it in, your teacher might give you a grace period of an extra day. If that happened, your teacher would be showing you extreme kindness. Grace and kindness go hand in hand. In Ephesians 2, Paul is telling us about the grace of Jesus who died on the cross to save us. In verse 7, it says, "in order that in the coming ages he might show the incomparable riches of his grace, expressed in his kindness to us in Christ Jesus." In this verse we learn that God's grace came through kindness to us from Jesus. This fruit of the Spirit is one that you will need to use every day. Always remember that your kindness needs to be filled with grace. The truth is, no one is perfect and everyone makes mistakes. There are people in this world that do not deserve kindness, which is why you need to be kind to them anyway, covered in grace.

Look up Ephesians 2:8-9 and write it here:

When has someone shown you kindness through grace? When have you shown graceful kindness to others?

Daily Challenge:

Think of someone you will be with soon that is mean or unfair to you. Decide now that you will go out of your way to show them grace and be kind. How will you do it, what will you do, and what do you hope the result will be?

Day 20

Christ-like Kindness

Kindness works by putting God and other people before yourself. It is often becoming selfless instead of selfish and nice instead of treating people how they might treat you. Kindness is not based on how you feel about yourself or someone else; kindness is based on how you feel about God as you try to copy how Jesus treated other people.

In Titus 3:4-5, we see that it was out of the kindness of God that Jesus came. If you ever want to know how to act towards other people, look at the way Jesus acted in that situation. Jesus healed people out of kindness, he helped people out of his loving kindness, and He taught people in kindness and grace. In Luke 10, Jesus tells the story of the Good Samaritan. This is the ultimate example of kindness. These men did not know each other, and many would say they were enemies. After telling this story, Jesus says in Luke 10:37, "Go, and do likewise." You can never go wrong with treating other people with Christ-like kindness.

Look up Titus 3:4-5 and write it here:

Is it hard for you to show kindness to all people? Who do you have an easy time showing kindness to and why? Who do you have a hard time showing kindness to and why?

Daily Challenge:
Look up Luke 10:25-37 and read the whole story of the Good Samaritan.

Day 21

Kind Nest

Sometimes it is easier to be kind to friends at school than family members in your home. This may be true for you and your brother/sister and parents. The truth is, we are to be kind to everyone, from those we are closest to all the way to those we don't like. Why, because kindness is a fruit of the Spirit, and it is a sign that you value your relationship with Jesus. In 2 Corinthians 6:6 we read, "We prove ourselves by our purity, our understanding, our patience, our kindness, by the Holy Spirit within us, and by our sincere love" (NLT). How can we prove these things are in us if we do not live them out to the people we are closest to? Your home is your nest. It is the place that you live and grow the most. Prove to yourself and to God that the fruit of the Spirit is important to you by bringing kindness into your home and making it your kind nest.

Re-write 2 Corinthians 6:6 and underline all the important words in that verse.

Why is it hard to be kind to the people you know and love the most?

Daily Challenge:
Set a goal for how to bring kindness to your family. List every family member below, and one thing you can do to be kind to them.

Day 22

Kind Clothing

As everyone knows, the clothes you wear are important. You have certain kinds of clothing for specific occasions. For example, if you are going swimming, you wear a swimsuit. If you are attending a wedding, you will dress up more than if you are playing outside with friends. Your clothes help you prepare for what it is that you are about to do. In Colossians 3:12, we read, "Therefore, as God's chosen people, holy and dearly loved, clothe yourselves with compassion, kindness, humility, gentleness and patience." This verse uses the word "clothe" for a very good reason. These five characteristics are important to your walk with Christ, and they all relate to a fruit of the Spirit. To clothe yourself with kindness means to wake up every morning and dress yourself to be kind that day, much like you dress yourself for school. By doing this, you will commit to wearing kindness on your shoulders all day as people see your kindness just as evident as the shirt on your back.

Re-write Colossians 3:12 and underline all the important words in that verse.

How do you feel when a friend is kind to you?

Daily Challenge:
Pray for a spirit of unending kindness in your life. Ask God to remind you every day to be kind, and then put your commitment of kindness to the test.

Day 23

Acts of Kindness

In the book of Acts, we read about Paul and his travels to share the Gospel. In Acts 27, Paul's ship gets caught in a major storm, and he is shipwrecked on an island. He is lost, hungry, and far from home. He is in need of kindness. In Acts 28:2 we read, "The islanders showed us unusual kindness. They built a fire and welcomed us all because it was raining and cold." This act of kindness would have given Paul a renewed spirit in his faith.

Every day, there are people all around you who are in need of your kindness. You often do not know what someone is dealing with when you meet them, but it never hurts to give them unusual kindness. This includes people at school, the server at the restaurant, and people you pass by on the street. For Paul, the kindness showed by the island people led him and his crew to heal many of the sick on the island. In verse 10 it says, "They honored us in many ways; and when we were ready to sail, they furnished us with the supplies we needed." It was kindness that started as a small ripple and turned into a large wave of blessing that benefited everyone on the island.

Read Acts 28:1-10 and make a list of all the blessings caused by the islanders' first act of kindness.

How have you seen one act of kindness start a ripple effect of blessings that made a significant impact on you and other people?

Daily Challenge:
What are five things you can do to cause a storm of blessings through one act of kindness?

Day 24

God is Good

The next fruit of the Spirit is goodness, which is the pursuit of doing good. Goodness is related to what we would call Godliness because God is our ultimate example of what is good. When you were a child, you might have said the prayer, "God is great, God is good, let us thank Him for our food." God is good, and He is our example of knowing what is good and having goodness. Throughout the Psalms we read that God is good. One of those verses is Psalm 119:68 which asks God to teach us how to be good. There is no better way to learn goodness than to learn it from God Himself. As you spend the next five days learning more about this Fruit of the Spirit, ask God to show you what it means to pursue goodness in your life.

Look up Psalm 119:68 and write it here:

What are some ways in which God is good?

Daily Challenge:
Spend some time looking up these verses on God's
goodness:
Psalms 107:1   Psalms 145:9
Psalms 84:11   Psalms 34:8

Day 25

Good Doer

The way to develop the goodness fruit of the Spirit is to do good to others. Think of it this way, God is good and his goodness is given to you to do good to others. Galatians 6:10 is an important verse for understanding this. First, it describes the way that we are to do good when we have the opportunity. It does not say that we do good when we feel like it or when we want to impress someone. It says that if God gives you the opportunity to do good, you need to take advantage of that. Secondly, it says that we should do good to all people. So, who does that leave out? Does that mean everyone except the person you don't like? Is it saying to do good to everyone except your brother or sister? It says everyone. Then it further explains that we are to do good especially to those who are Christians. Now, it is already clear that you are to do good to everyone when given the chance, so this verse is not saying that your goodness is only for believers. One of the reasons it emphasizes doing good to other believers is so you can set an example for how to be a doer of goodness, so all Christians will see your fruit and learn to do good themselves.

Look up Galatians 6:10 and write it here:

What are some examples of doing good to others?

Daily Challenge:
Take the examples you listed above and think about how you will live out goodness to others this week.

Day 26

Good Talk

Living out goodness is not only about what you do, but also about what you say. Maybe you have heard the old saying, "Sticks and stones can break my bones, but words will never hurt me." That could not be more false because words can sometimes hurt worse than sticks and stones. When we talk down to someone or talk about someone behind their back, we are not doing good. Ephesians 4:29 says, "Do not let any unwholesome talk come out of your mouths…". When something is unwholesome, it is not whole. It is broken and bad. When your words are whole, they are truthful and encouraging to other people. The verse goes on to say that our words need to build people up and not bring them down. This goes back to the Golden Rule found in Matthew 7:12, "Do to others whatever you would like them to do to you." If you don't want people saying negative things to you, don't say negative things. If you want others to encourage you, be an encourager. Speak in such a way that others will be lifted up by your words so that it will impact their own belief in Jesus.

Look up Ephesians 4:29 and write it here:

How does it make you feel when people speak
wholesome words to you?

Daily Challenge:
Write out five sentences of encouragement that you could
say to someone to speak goodness to them.

Day 27

Of Good Character

Do you know what character is? In a movie, a character is the person in the story, played by an actor. In life, character is the condition of your nature as a person. That might be confusing, so let me explain. Compare two people: first you have a Christian girl who always wants to help people in need, and the other is a guy who breaks into stores to steal money. The girl is of good character because she has chosen to do what is right. The man does not have a good nature, or character, because he hurts others for his own gain. In 1 Corinthians 15:33, the Bible says, "Do not be misled: 'Bad company corrupts good character.'" When it says, "bad company," it means that having friends with a bad character will keep you from having a good character. When you allow goodness to bloom and blossom in you, you will make good decisions and your character will be filled with goodness as well. It is important for all Christians to have a good reputation so that your witness is worthy of sharing. So remember, be of good character.

Look up 1 Timothy 4:12 and write it here:

Looking at the verse you just wrote above, how is setting a good example in your works, love, faith, and purity a good way to develop a good character?

Daily Challenge:
What is one way you can set a good example in speech, love, faith, and purity?

Day 28

The Good Way

Have you ever had to make a decision, but you were not sure which way to go? Only one choice will lead you in the right direction, but you are not sure which decision to make. In Jeremiah 6:16, we see a process for how to determine the right decision. First it says to stand at the crossroads and look. This refers to the crossroad of your decision. Look around and see if there is an obvious answer. Then it says to ask. This means to pray. You are to pray for the good way, which is the Godly way. This is the way God wants you to go. The next step is to actually walk in the direction of the good way, which is the most important step. Then, the verse says, you will find rest for your soul. This is important because your soul is your spiritual self, and you do not want a restless soul. If you want peace in your life, you will search the good way, walk in it, and find rest that only God can give.

Look up Jeremiah 6:16 and write it here:

Why is it important to take the time you need to find the good path to follow in life?

Daily Challenge:
Think of a decision that you need to make (or will have to make) and go through the directions in this verse to outline your steps.

Look around and see if there is an obvious answer.

Pray about the right decision.

Pray that God will lead you to the good way.

Walk in the good way and find rest for your soul.

Day 29

Gentle Like Jesus

When you hear the word "gentleness", what do you think of? Do you think of a person who is kind and considerate or someone who is soft and weak? If you said the first option, you are right. Our example for all of the spiritual fruits is Jesus, and Jesus had gentleness. But trust me, Jesus was not soft and weak.

There are many places in the Gospels that speak of the gentleness of Jesus. He was always gentle in the way He dealt with hurting and needy people and in the way He related to His close friends. In 2 Corinthians 10:1, Paul says, "Now I, Paul, myself urge you by the meekness and gentleness of Christ…" He is saying that he is gentle with the people he is writing to because Jesus used gentleness with people. In Matthew 11:29, Jesus says that he is gentle and that we can come to him with our heavy needs. I hope in the next two days you will learn what gentleness is and how to be gentle like Jesus.

Look up Matthew 11:29 and write it here:

Describe how someone with gentleness treats people.

Daily Challenge:
Think about an example of when you used gentleness and an example of when you might use it in the future.

Day 30

Visibly Gentle

A person that is gentle is someone who is kind and tender hearted. This means that they have compassion for other people. The word compassion is a compound word, meaning that it comes from two words. Passion means to love, and the prefix "com" means together with. To have compassion means to care for someone where they are. To see someone in need and have compassion is not just to have pity on them but to put yourself in their shoes and feel the hurt that they feel. Compassion is an essential part of showing gentleness. In Philippians 4:5, it says that your gentleness must be so real that it is seen by those around you. When you see someone in need and you walk past them and give them a dollar, you might be helping them, but you are not showing gentleness. But, if you stop and talk with them, hear them out, and learn how you can best meet their needs, you have made your gentleness visible.

Look up Philippians 4:5 and write it here:

What other fruits of the Spirit do you think are included in making gentleness visible?

Daily Challenge:
Think of a situation in your life where you could show gentleness to others. Create a plan for how you will act when that scenario happens.

Day 31

Stuck-on Humility

There is one personal attribute that must be in your life if you are going to genuinely live out all the fruit of the Spirit, and that is humility. Humility is an act of putting yourself behind others. It is directly opposite to looking at yourself proudly and thinking that you are better than any one else. We have already talked about Colossians 3:12 in the section on kindness, but I want you to see how humility is active with the other fruit of the Spirit. Colossians 3:12 says, "Therefore, as God's chosen people, holy and dearly loved, clothe yourselves with compassion, kindness, humility, gentleness and patience." I like how Paul put humility in the middle as if to say that being humble is the glue that keeps the others stuck together. If you want to develop a gentle heart, you must focus on being humble because it is impossible to have compassion for others when you are centered on yourself.

Look up James 4:10 and write it here:

Look at the verse you just wrote (James 4:10). What does that verse mean to you?

Daily Challenge:
Think about a few situations where you might be tempted to be less than humble (playing a sport you are good at, performing in something that is easy to you, etc). How will you focus on humility the next time you are doing that activity?

Day 32

Full of Faith

The next fruit of the Spirit is faithfulness. Faith is trusting in God, no matter what. Faith is believing that everything God has ever said is true. Faithfulness has been given to us as a spiritual fruit because we will need it to get through the hardest moments of life.

The Bible has a lot to say about being faithful. First, Ephesians 2:8 reminds us that it is through faith that God has saved us. It is through believing in God that gives us eternal life. Secondly, Proverbs 28:20 says that "A faithful person will be richly blessed," because following God's direction in life will always lead to a full life. Thirdly, the Bible tells us that we must have faith, or we can not please God. Hebrews 11:6 says, "And without faith it is impossible to please him, for whoever would draw near to God must believe that he exists and that he rewards those who seek him." Faithfulness is very important to your relationship with Jesus. Being faithful means to be full of faith.

Look up Ephesians 2:8 and write it here:

In your own words, what are the three points about faithfulness in the Bible that was shared above?

Daily Challenge:
Think about a time that you showed faithfulness to God. Write it below so that you will remember that example of your faithfulness. If you can not think of a time, try to remember the next moment of faithfulness in your life and come back to write it here.

Day 33

Fear Not

The opposite of faith is fear. Fear will always distract you from focusing on your faithfulness. But God wants you to be faithful, not fearful. In John 14:27, Jesus says, "Do not let your hearts be troubled and do not be afraid." Do you know how many days there are in a year? If you said, "365" you are right. Do you know how many times the Bible says, "Do not fear,"? If you guessed, 365, you are right again. This is so important to God that He gave us a new verse every day to remind us not to be fearful. So why do you think people are afraid? The answer is because we doubt. Doubt is the feeling we get when we are afraid and unsure of something. But the Bible tells us to be strong and to remember that God is always with us. All you have to do is pray and ask God to give you that strength. In James 1:6, it says, "But let him ask in faith, with no doubting, for the one who doubts is like a wave of the sea that is driven and tossed by the wind." Do not fear, but instead have faith.

Look up Isaiah 41:10 and write it here:

List all the reasons you can think of for why Christian people have fear and doubt.

Daily Challenge:
Make a commitment to yourself today that you will live in faith and not fear. This does not mean you will never be scared, but instead of doubting, you will pray for strength. Write out a commitment to be faithful and not fearful.

Day 34

God's Faithfulness

We can be faithful to God because God is faithful to us. As Psalm 100:4-5 tells us, God's faithfulness is great, and it continues for all time. Maybe you have heard the old song that comes from the verse of Lamentations 3:23 that says, "Great is your faithfulness." Jesus promises that he will never leave us, and it is very important that we never forget that. Satan will try very hard to convince you that God is not faithful, but you know better than that. In 2 Thessalonians 3:3, we read that "The Lord is faithful, and he will strengthen and protect you from the evil one." It is because of God's faithfulness that we can be in a relationship with Jesus. The Bible assures us of this in 1 Corinthians 1:9, and we can believe that it is true.

Look up 1 Corinthians 1:9 and write it here:

In what ways is God faithful to you?

Daily Challenge:
Make a list of how you can be more faithful to God
because of His faithfulness to you.

Day 35

Faithful in Prayer

One way that we can be faithful to God is to be faithful in prayer. The truth is, God wants to have a relationship with you. He wants to know you and help you live your life to the fullest. One of the ways this happens is to grow deeper by learning to be faithful in your prayer life. The Bible says a lot about prayer. Colossians 4:2 tells us to be devoted or committed to prayer. Jeremiah 29:12 reminds us that God will always listen to our prayers, and in Romans 12:12 we are told to be faithful in prayer. As you know, faithfulness is a fruit of the Spirit, and the more committed we are to God, the more faithful we will be to Him. Being faithful in prayer is to be active and honest in prayer. Being active in prayer means to pray all the time. In 1 Thessalonians 5:16, we are told to pray without stopping which means to always have the attitude of prayer in your heart. To be honest in your prayers is to tell God everything and never hold anything back. If you are afraid, then tell God. If you need help, God wants to know. If you are mad, happy, sad, or confused, talk to God and tell Him how you feel. Even though He already knows your thoughts, He wants to hear it from you, as you trust that He will be faithful to you as you are faithful to Him.

Look up Romans 12:12 and write it here:

Do you think praying often is hard or easy to do? List reasons why you think that.

Daily Challenge:
Write out a prayer to God below. If you have never written a prayer, you might find that it is a powerful thing to do. Feel free to tell God everything you want to tell Him, and don't forget to praise Him and pray for others, too.

Day 36

Mountain Moving

How hard do you think it would be to walk up to a large mountain and push it an inch or two? Is that possible? In Matthew 17:20, Jesus said something very strange. He said that if we only could have faith as big as a mustard seed, then we could move a large mountain. A mustard seed is one of the smallest seeds you can find, and Jesus said that someone with faith as small as one of those seeds could move a mountain. Do you think you could move a mountain with faith? Do you think God could? The truth is, the power we have because of our faith is actually God's power. We trust in God, and we become strong in his strength. As Philippians 4:13 tells us, "I can do all things through Christ who gives me strength." The most important words of this verse is not "I" or "things" or even "strength." The most important words of that verse is "through Christ." Our strength and faithfulness come through Christ, and it is only when we trust Him that we have power. In Matthew 25, Jesus tells a story of a man with three workers. He trusts each worker with part of his wealth while he is gone and asks them to invest it. When the man returns home, he says to the workers who did a good job: "Well done, good and faithful servant. You have been faithful over a little; I will set you over much. Enter into the joy of your master," (Matthew 25:21). It is because those workers were faithful with what God gave them that allowed them to do God's will and be successful.

Look up Matthew 17:20 and write it here:

What is a big "mountain" (large prayer need) in your life that you need God's help to move? Think about it and write it below.

Daily Challenge:
The challenge is to take a week (or more) and pray every time you think about the "mountain" that you listed above.

Day 37

Control Your Self

The final fruit of the Spirit is self-control. To have self-control is to be disciplined and able to keep yourself from doing wrong things. In Titus 1:8, a follower of Christ is referred to as someone who is "hospitable, one who loves what is good, who is self-controlled, upright, holy and disciplined." To be self-controlled is to be in control of your self, which is easier to say than to do. Think of self-control like the protective walls of a city. If the wall is secure, then the people will be safe. If the wall is broken, then it will be easy for the enemy to come in and invade. Self-control is like the walls of your life, protecting you from getting off course in your pursuit of living for God. In Proverbs 25:28, we read, "Like a city whose walls are broken through is a person who lacks self-control." Learn to develop self-control, and you will learn to grow deeper in your faith and walk with Christ. Don't let your walls crack.

Look up Romans 12:2 and write it here:

What does Romans 12:2 have to do with self-control?

Daily Challenge:
List all the "holes" in your wall (or things you do not
have self-control in) that you can think of, and commit to
developing control over those things, so you can be more
disciplined in your life.

Day 38

Control Your Mind

One of the ways that we develop self-control is to learn how to control our thinking. We can sin so much with our thinking that we can loose sight of what God wants for us in our lives. The way to control our minds is to control our thinking. Instead of thinking about bad things, we need to start thinking of good things. This might mean that we control what we see and hear. If we watch and listen to trash, we will begin to think about that trash. Colossians 3:2 tells us to think about Godly things instead of worldly things. In Ephesians 4:22-24, we are told "to be made new in the attitude of your minds; and to put on the new self, created to be like God in true righteousness and holiness." This is a daily prayer of asking God to renew our thinking. Here are three ways to control your mind. First, stop looking at and listening to things that will pull you way from your relationship with God. Next, fill your mind with things that are pleasing to God. Then, pray every day that God will help you control your mind. Then you will be able to live out the fruit of the Spirit in your life.

Look up Philippians 4:8 and write it here:

Look at the list of things to think about in Philippians 4:8. Write an example of each of them.

Daily Challenge:
List the things that are keeping you from controlling your mind (things you see, hear, say). Now, spend some time away from those things, and see if you have more self-control after a week or more.

Day 39

Control Your Mouth

You might not think that the words you say are important to living out the fruit of the Spirit, but they are critical. The truth is, your words have the power to encourage someone and the power to hurt people. When you develop self-control over your mouth, you will be able to be kind to those who need your kindness. In Colossians 4:6, it says that our conversations should always be filled with grace, and Ephesians 4:29 says, "Do not let any unwholesome talk come out of your mouths, but only what is helpful for building others up according to their needs, that it may benefit those who listen." In James 3, there is an example of how powerful our words can be. James compares our tongue to the rudder of a large ship. Compared to the ship, the rudder is tiny, but it is what controls and steers the boat. In the same way, our tongue is small, but it can control our whole body. The best way to control your words is to do what it says in 2 Corinthians 10:5 and take all of your thoughts captive. This means that before your thoughts become words, you capture them and determine if they are harmful or not. This takes discipline and self control, but I know you can do it.

Look up Colossians 4:6 and write it here:

Read James 3:3-6 and list the three comparisons that James makes for the tongue. How can each of them be dangerous? How can your words be just as bad?

Daily Challenge:
List as many encouraging words that you can think of, and then look over the list and try to use them all in the next few days.

Day 40

Control Your Fruit

Over the past 40 days you have been studying the fruit of the Spirit. These are all in you if you are following Jesus. But, as you know by now, just because they are in you doesn't mean that you are living them out. You must ultimately take control over the fruits in your life and let them grow. Self-control is important in order to live out the other fruits of the Spirit. For example, you can not have peace if you can not keep yourself from getting angry. You can not live out patience if you are always impatient. You can not be kind, loving, joyful, good, gentle, or faithful if you do not have self-control.

In John 15:5 Jesus tells us how to help these fruits grow in us. He said, "I am the vine; you are the branches. If you remain in me and I in you, you will bear much fruit; apart from me you can do nothing." Think of a large, healthy tree. God is the trunk, and you are the branch. If the branch is cut off from the tree, then it will die. If it stays connected, it will bear fruit. You are that branch. You must stay connected to God in order to bear fruit. This means you need to live the way God instructs you to live in Scripture. If you take control over keeping your life spiritually healthy, you will grow rich fruit that will change the world around you. But, just like Jesus said, apart from this, you will do nothing. The opportunity is yours, and I know you can do it. You would not have made it to the end of this book if you didn't have a deep desire to grow in your relationship with Christ. Now, go out there and bear much fruit.

Look up John 15:8 and write it here:

What does it mean to you to stay connected to the trunk of Jesus and bear lots of fruit?

Daily Challenge:
Now that you have finished the book, what are you going to do to continue to grow in your faith and continue to bear fruit? Write your answer on the next page.